Meet my neighbor, the restaurant owner

Marc Crabtree
Author and Photographer

🌳 Crabtree Publishing Company

www.crabtreebooks.com

☘ Crabtree Publishing Company

Meet my neighbor, the restaurant owner

For William and Cindy, with thanks

Author and photographer
Marc Crabtree

Editor
Reagan Miller

Proofreaders
Corey Long
Crystal Sikkens

Design
Samantha Crabtree

Production coordinator
Margaret Amy Salter

Photographs
All photographs by Marc Crabtree except:
Shutterstock: pages 3, 24 (softball)

Library and Archives Canada Cataloguing in Publication

Crabtree, Marc
    Meet my neighbor, the restaurant owner / Marc Crabtree, author
and photographer.

(Meet my neighbor)
ISBN 978-0-7787-4576-1 (bound).--ISBN 978-0-7787-4586-0 (pbk.)

    1. Wong, William, 1971- --Juvenile literature. 2. Restaurateurs--
Canada--Biography--Juvenile literature. 3. Restaurant management--
Juvenile literature. I. Title. II. Series: Crabtree, Marc. Meet my neighbor.

TX910.5.W65C73 2010   j647.95092   C2009-906788-9

Library of Congress Cataloging-in-Publication Data

Crabtree, Marc.
 Meet my neighbor, the restaurant owner / author and photographer,
Marc Crabtree.
      p. cm. -- (Meet my neighbor)
  ISBN 978-0-7787-4576-1 (reinforced lib. bdg. : alk. paper) --
  ISBN 978-0-7787-4586-0 (pbk. : alk. paper)
  1. Food service--Juvenile literature. 2. Restaurateurs--Juvenile
literature. I. Title. II. Series.

 TX943.C73 2010
 647.95092--dc22

                                                    2009047088

Crabtree Publishing Company

www.crabtreebooks.com   1-800-387-7650

Printed in the USA/122009/CG20091120

Published in Canada
Crabtree Publishing
616 Welland Ave.
St. Catharines, Ontario
L2M 5V6

Published in the United States
Crabtree Publishing
PMB 59051
350 Fifth Avenue, 59th Floor
New York, New York 10118

Published in the United Kingdom
Crabtree Publishing
Maritime House
Basin Road North, Hove
BN41 1WR

Published in Australia
Crabtree Publishing
386 Mt. Alexander Rd.
Ascot Vale (Melbourne)
VIC 3032

Meet my Neighbor

Contents

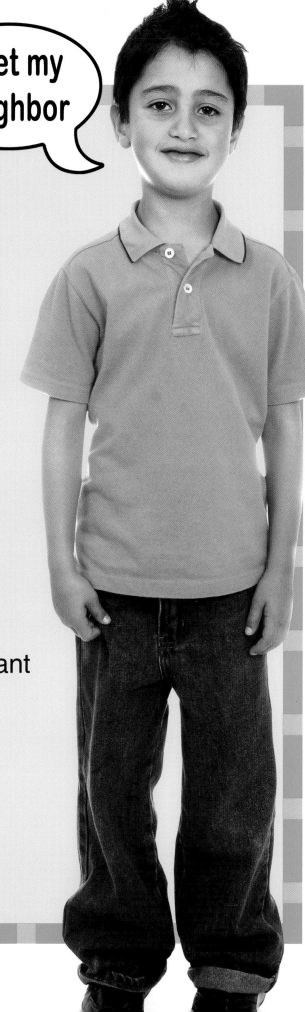

Meet my neighbor, William Wong, and his wife, Cindy.

Today, William and Cindy are moving into their new house.

William and Cindy got married a short time ago. They got married on a beautiful beach.

William works at his family's restaurant. William's father opened the restaurant more than 30 years ago.

William gives a customer's **food order** to a **cook**.

11

The cooks use fresh **ingredients** in all their recipes.

12

The cooks work together to make the food.

William takes a food order for delivery over the telephone.

William prepares a plate of chicken wings.

William helps a cook pack food for delivery.

15

When the restaurant is busy, William helps the cooks make the food.

Cindy also helps at the restaurant.

She serves the customers and clears dishes from the tables.

Cindy wipes the table clean for the next customer.

19

William loads dirty dishes into a large **dishwasher**.

This customer pays William for her meal.

William delivers food to a customer's home.

After work, William has fun playing **softball** with his friends.

William runs around the bases after hitting the softball.

This is William's softball team.

Glossary

food order

cook

ingredients

dishwasher

softball

Printed in the U.S.A. - CG